T0158583

Viva the Real

Jill Jones was born in Sydney and has lived in Adelaide since 2008. She has published ten full-length poetry books and a number of chapbooks, including *The Beautiful Anxiety*, which won the Victorian Premier's Literary Award for Poetry in 2015, and *Breaking the Days*, which won the Whitmore Press Manuscript Prize in 2014 and was shortlisted for the Kenneth Slessor Poetry Prize in 2017. She has also won the Kenneth Slessor Poetry Prize and the Mary Gilmore Award. Her work is published widely in Australian and international anthologies, magazines and periodicals, and has been translated into Chinese, Dutch, French, Italian, Czech, Macedonian and Spanish. She has worked as a film reviewer, journalist, book editor and arts administrator. In 2014 she was poet-in-residence at Stockholm University. She currently teaches at the University of Adelaide where she is also a member of the J.M. Coetzee Centre for Creative Practice.

ALSO BY JILL JONES

Brink
The Leaves Are My Sisters
Breaking the Days
The Beautiful Anxiety
Ash is Here, So are Stars
Dark Bright Doors
Senses Working Out
Speak Which: Hay(na)ku Poems
Broken/Open
Fold Unfold
Struggle and Radiance: Ten Commentaries
Where the Sea Burns
Screens Jets Heaven: New and Selected Poems
The Book of Possibilities
Flagging Down Time
The Mask and the Jagged Star

Jill Jones
Viva the Real

For Annette
'our hands gather'

First published 2018 by University of Queensland Press
PO Box 6042, St Lucia, Queensland 4067 Australia

uqp.com.au
uqp@uqp.uq.edu.au

Copyright © Jill Jones 2018
The moral rights of the author have been asserted.

This book is copyright. Except for private study, research, criticism or
reviews, as permitted under the *Copyright Act*, no part of this book may be
reproduced, stored in a retrieval system, or transmitted in any form or by
any means without prior written permission. Enquiries should be made to
the publisher.

Cover design by Sandy Cull, gogoGingko
Author photograph by Annette Willis
Typeset in 11.5/14pt Garamond by Post Pre-press Group, Brisbane
Printed in Australia by McPherson's Printing Group, Melbourne

The University of Queensland Press is
assisted by the Australian Government
through the Australia Council, its arts
funding and advisory body.

A catalogue record for this
book is available from the
National Library of Australia

ISBN 978 0 7022 6010 0 (pbk)
ISBN 978 0 7022 6136 7 (pdf)
ISBN 978 0 7022 6137 4 (epub)
ISBN 978 0 7022 6138 1 (kindle)

University of Queensland Press uses papers that are natural, renewable
and recyclable products made from wood grown in sustainable forests.
The logging and manufacturing processes conform to the
environmental regulations of the country of origin.

Contents

The Make-Do

The day drops voices
on my tongue, all the burnt dust,
garbage, tenderness. Duties waste time.

I am stupid among crisp brown leaves.
I lick salt fresh from the window
and wait for the big moon.

I get more curious than you think.
Change is impure, vulgar,
a magnificent rush in make-do.

Dust sticks to my daydream shoes.
A taxi revs its autonomy and escapes
into a dirty, unclear horizon.

The main road is a dream hatched,
a tremendous streaking
in the fast fold of fret lines.

I can't always dash moments.
I haunt my junk.

The River Night

All the old words are new words
aligned in a shaky way
all over the climbing sheet,
shanks of curtains, the crispy cords.

Now they wind me up
and work free in planet light,
the risky tintinnabulation
of vine, and tree, and thorn.

The night is always green.
It's a flaky field of beat folly
and fishy streams,
jittery laps of unfinished work.

It's the hour of lust and rain.
What do you do with lust and rain?
Drink and wander and shiver.
Hey, sometimes it's all river.

Some thing laughs its dream.
Some thing swims above.
Some thing sheds its smoke.
Some thing runs.

I'm so afraid that I want to joke
in an hour of ardent seconds.
New words rain like love,
earth shaking its light, its weather.

I unfasten a thousand sheets.
I risk the river.
I find something patient
among wandering exhaust and sap.

Swoop

smell dirt under tongues as worms
    loop over
    leaf syllables
big fat jazz blowing blossom, dogs
    politics, scraps
    climate! hear it roar
fretting along gutters and roads
    sign says 'gobble and go'
    but where
we're all sung under the flush of
    pollen
    a day's leavings
how old is the gate, listen to it swing
    weather grips
    your clothes
how lucky! as if that's all there is
    glimpse of
    water through trees
leaves break in your hand, wing swoop
    syncopates
    blues of the galaxy
huge chords rush outside, rain, trucks
    hard dreams
    three stars in a pool

the grass shivers

Temper

They say morning's temper
binds you to this world
of taking. As if the air said
all you need is to scram
or laugh. If it's real payback,
why try to earn it.
There are better things to do
with your shoes.
This is no mystery.
Movement chafes expectancy
till it hurts and hackles.
It's a pissing contest,
round that hew
the hours hand you.
You can't whimper.
This, also, isn't a mystery.
It's halfway day.
The dog's at the fence.

The Storm

The storm catches on the door.
It's a good sign, a surge that's more than breathing,
that blows away dirt from reliquaries,
and directions from their careful signs.
It's near speech and near trembling,
sky-bringer fate crowning from its centre,
if there was a centre rather than millennia
of waves, segmentation, volcanic chemistry.
And all this chlorophyll blowing around,
that does not understand solitude
but certainly vortex and rage,
the made and unmade clouds, constant phantoms
and caprices, the moving walls.
There is no void.   There is future,
no matter which way breaks,
the branch we find fallen on the new plants.
It's not a lucky escape from death, rust, abrasion,
    or bad thoughts
as I revise the possibilities within milliseconds.
A second doesn't describe any thought.
A thought doesn't show how I might want to run.
Time has nothing to do with what I hope to find
trembling in a gauge or written on a screen.
What passes is passing, and will pass.
If anything is eternal it is the motion,
as I step out to sweep what has gone and come.
The leaves make a noise almost as if
I was waiting for someone.

The Sex of the House

Watching morning from the inside
    The approximate spills on your skin
Answering a phone in a dream
    And you pick it up as light strikes
      And so on

It's not your heart that's the bird
    Your guts flutter in spring
The bumpy road to the interior
    That's where it's all happening

Something drips in the ceiling
    And underneath evidence of love
Of leavings, stovetops, nails
    Catching on the old ghost you asked to leave

Why are there no crisp mornings
    Why can't I walk among citizens
Stop slamming the door
    Instead of dreaming of the holy

What was it you wanted to tell me
    On a phone, in a dream
In a country that doesn't exist
    Where we could live and even die
      And so on

Rituals in Ultrasound and Gardens

What worlds we incorporate
in body time which is where
those worlds are entranced
in entering flesh darkness
on the screen numb pain
mirrored through sound
that seems chaotic but is
knitted in bodied work

How does form work?
The spread of a woman's shape
more than voice echo in
being that crater that mere
that long hill that internal
swallowed light the shiver of
breath in darkness that is also
being pale bone dark muscle
the lake of torso brown
and pink mouths of pleasure to eat
and drink to touch skin like
a mirror a spiral or winglike
as if flight was possible

To escape the human for a
moment like being a rock or
a leaf, a mist, a serpent, a door as
proximities stream nerve light
glare of the lungs and heart
glimmer of spine tallow of
absences or spaces as if almost
casual about blood glyph

A moment in a wave of thought
lucid and fuzzy together
nothing is ever still   an assembly
like history, scenes, weaving
undulant seas, savannas, freeways
peeling bark, dying trees, masked power
soft power spreading into
fissures of markets and parliaments
impressions in layers of rock
ghost shapes in metal, graveyards
as gardens, housings spirited
in vined, veined leafy fresh dermis
shaped as a woman shapes

Maps and Cavities

Something crackles   under my left heel
    the green floor
    the white dust

Weeds ferment

I'm stumbling on autopilot
all my artefacts
        are wrapped in decisions
my headache splashes   out

The afternoon shadow   on the fence
        is dependable

The sky is busy
there are cavities   for the wind

Music doesn't   always
make it right

Sometimes the ground
    shakes   slightly
    as though my feet shiver
    It's a racket, the earth

What did we do   when it was quiet
It has never
    been quiet

Orders of chaos   make syllables sweet

There are marks all over the water
There's water all over the water

Pain is an   all day thing
sometimes
     things improve

Streets crack   in the century
cold lowers
     onto the square

The yonder is crazy

Look at the stars
Watch birds
Think about   old migrations
Fail again
Think about new migrations   again

Walls fill with   ardent discussion
each word
loving   each word

The present   seems to have passed
the pain in my shoulder
     remains

Planes loop past the moon

Every day something's added
        to the floor
the hidden rises
    plastic, metal
    forgotten things
    blooms

Someone's knocking   on the door
there's probably an answer

Neglect archetypes   make an escape

The air   is hissing

The Blossoms of Retail

We become our shopping
something that's not quite feeling
a semi-emotion as if underwater
or near tears unable to breathe or drown.

Are we living in the present
tense or another kind of mood?
Where are the horses, the plains?
All is now the ting machine
like hearts and minds living
diffidently with eyes closed.

Tiredness streams in the
supermarket's eyes, all of this
heaviness on shelves
shrink-wrap cackling.

There are dry leaves everywhere
bursting in the doors
over the white floor
perpetual death and life entwined
like insect swarms, webs, cords.

The weights of money and goods
topple against our hide, our putty
skins, our plastic dresses, over our gritty
eyes, the smoke in our torsos
abdomens, our breasts all sexual desires
melting around our knees
packages of frozen meat, spiderlike
movements over our buttocks, tattoos
on our ankles in the shape of wings
but faded, distended.

We should be laughing instead
of wandering like evaporated luck
or a plot of bewilderments on price tags
sliding doors into the great cavern of the centre
full of gems, gowns, movie tricks.

And exit signs stretch out like
a system, a straight-seeming system
that is soon a dead end, a locked door
in the shape of wings but faded.

Mouth Song

I ate the song
I ate the telephone booth
I ate the tax form
the guidelines and the injunction.
I swallowed the driveway
all the neighbourhood watch
pamphlets, I ate the periodic table
statutes, another postal survey.

My taste has not improved
though I hear the elements singing
they have always been singing
they sing through fear
and counterfeits, wigs and seals
leaching of great caverns
of earth, they are
accounting in their fashion
vibrating like wine or coconut
spitting quarter rhymes and semi-light.

I walk towards home
tongue in its sweet with the music on
each rib in its own sky
each sky in its own key
and changing all my money
for directions, changing all my
positions as I go.

My Daylight Savings

It's that time of year
                         but gardens continue.
Here I am with a bucket and hose
                        in the front yard
as another train passes to Seaford or Tonsley.
Even poets and friends sometimes pass here, in various directions:
                        Peter and Lisa, on bikes,
or today Ken strolls by, walking Pola
                        and she's into the hedge
sniffing a dead bird, a bit of one.
Ken looks good, they've been
                        in Tasmania.
The EAF has some performance art happening:
'You should check it out. They
                        paid a lot of money for it.'

A garden is performance art
                        part conceptual, part organic.
You could see STC and Duchamp
                        arguing over the dying lawn:
'best grass in the best order', 'but grass
                        doesn't interest me, here's a suitcase'.
The bees don't care, flowers are ready-mades always
                        for their not-so-secret ministry.

'All Nature seems at work.'
But I'm erasing aphids with my thumb
                       and ants with my boots
or spilling precious water onto the path.
               I am not a good soul even on Sunday.
Another killer, just like the birds
                 cute and useless like a lot of exotics.

They say it's cold in Sydney, and raining.
                         Well, bully for them.
We water by the bucketload
               and the dams dry up
                    under high blue skies.
But, nope, here's the clouds again
           that covered up much of the eclipse last night,
               the plum tree rains down
its mellow fruitfulness
               its dark red leaves – it's a turning.

We perform tasks
            turn back clocks, the wind
                  moves things around.
We move things around.
Does anyone really know what time it is?

It all sounds like paper
                mixing language with
                                sounds of Sunday.
Gábor Szabó mixes his
                      60s gipsy pop jazz through
                                my tinny speakers
reminding me of clothes
                      I could never wear
                                attitudes I somehow never believed.

And though it's Easter, the chocolate's gone
                so has the blood moon
                      and the air's lost its heat.
Yusef Lateef's flute sounds as if
                    it's got it right
                              airy performance, a kind
of dance, fingers across bamboo
                    conceptual bamboo, but also organic
                        making sounds
improvising but in tune
                      and in time with
                            so many things.

Bad Sphere Dust-up

shallow duty
  shell government
    bad sphere

hormone lineage
  beastly charmer
    sexist dustbin

househunter loam
  sheet spleen
    bad spider

horoscope liner
  bairn spew
    shag chatterbox

menaced dunce-hat
  lawn mephisto
    bad spoof

lap maintenance
  shapeless self
    language mainland

bad cheese
  shelf gospel
    mateship dust-up

laughter majority
  sheep shift
bad cheque

layabout self-starter
  bastard spice
shelter stress

hospital liquidity
  selfless gasbag
bad childhood

baffled spendthrift
  horny linen
shackled stopgap

bad creature
  share earth
shake gloat

My Sceptic Tremor

Perhaps I require revolution rather than mending day
or need to get back to my ill channels,
disinterest, a fetish or two
and a more obvious sin than procrastination.
Force is never equal, not in my calculations,
nor is severance or servitude.

I tell myself lies that sound like truths. That's clever.
I turn out my pockets for dust, coins,
and palaver. That's too clever.

When I divide it evenly, the cavalry will come
with their shiny tear gas and lucrative immortality.
When I hold it out, the futurists will come
with their holograms and plebiscites, their ghastly chums
full of gosh and ingratitude.
When I hide it away, it will be covered up by
brazen vote cards and gaudy guilt.

Here are my stupid boots, my placards, a little book
of tasteful green catechism. Already the rocks hate me,
the wind turns its back, the day sours,
wearing out my slang, my tokens, my renewables,
the hopeless gluten between my bones, my brawn
and its wasteland of humours.

The only way to revolve is to stand still, give up my axis.
There's nothing special in that, except when
ground shudders or the wind refuses to hold me.

Even now my shoes fill with doubt and slick.
I can't mend, I can't fly but at least I can keep
sceptic tremor over so much prior glut.
Shame is my sticky thing.

Recovery Ward

The day is an experiment with scars
I smell of that knitting
Other machines zoom with their petroleum
and cogs of musk churn
Afternoon falls like a seed
A seed falls because it must
Autumn falls

My smallest scar puts out signals
Leaves scrape in tune
There's a shiver that precedes the eternal gust
I am missing something
the air can't replace
Between my body is between
A corpse flaps like thought

If they had given me wings
If I was more than holes
If I could contain the sigh or the scream
If I repaid ground with my rusty skin
I'd raise myself in my season

There is no self-help now
I can only speak in blood tongue
And let all the knots pull me through

Dream Design

is possibility   beyond
         the floor
wild windows   where you see
         and blow away
fancy closets   abandoned conceits

    or dream designs with
lintels   nails   gambrels   skirting boards
         at play
that spool and dash within

and whatever follows – the continual
         am

Headaches, a Goofy Taste

I can't show you exactly
but here somewhere
in my shoulder
that somehow connects
the flowers are heavy
paths curvaceous
tenderised smelling
of raisins, air blends
in your goofy cavities
and you become
unctuous, winsome
Someone, test me
not for clarity but not unlike
the things we do for
shove with honey on the sores
rust and yeast
washed from domains
and parklands into gutters
bituminous cracks
headaches timetables unlocking
in chromosomes and footsteps
inconstants established
in formulae, in fever
Taste me, lurching
into the rain

Poem Diesel Butterfly

The Wanderer Butterfly drifts
lands just beyond me
then rises
turns so
swift

Poetry actually does things
turns things
through the head ear page

   'Try that again.'
syllable by
sound by sound
learning to count, magically

Language is a replica
like a market
Choose your words
   or does the poem choose you

Diesel infiltrates from the street
the noise of grading
a footpath

Clearing my throat means
something, clusters
of phrases
echo, guttural or charm

re-
   present
        even when sad
or distracted

The Wanderer appears again
taking no note of me
I think three syllables
but it's already gone
before I smile

I taste the bitter gas
New gutters must be laid
for important works

I hope we can still breathe

The Variances

looking for ways to write back losses
I camp out waiting for a verdict
yellow drips into me

                my left hand shakes uncontrollably
            some days find me with the lucky wafer
              a walk to the back fence can be long

high moon in late blue sky
only halfway coming into its sphere
petals shrivel eventually

                everything smells of sap
                  the world is a vegetable
                  its pollen marks my sleeves

if exactitude is a virtue
my head spins
even the district seems insufficient

                birds are crazy and click fences
           there's a warning attached to clouds
              it's precise if you can ever read it

rain scatters in minutes
and hours remain dry
the open garden is full of stories

                my eyes haven't blown up
          heat sits all round like a fat chance
              I have medication forever

a position is like work
or a guest who pulls your life together
it becomes another question, doesn't it?

                              everything must be examined
                         though every day is simply a sample
                              even if it falls, even as it fails

now I'm slippery like defeat
pressure is apparent in what doesn't happen
in one leap, one door knock, the click of officials

                                   again, nothing happens
                                 there, it's happening again
                              it's chancy, speculative, foolish

money ineffably shines
a guitar sings in an elevator
what is it about the sound of the room?

                       the amazing walls, the insects, the choir
                          what of crows in tender temperatures?
                                   perhaps there are alternatives

go back into years and check the papers
in the world of reunions there's a world of grudges
weather catches on the window

                              like a horizon with a demand
                              a lure on the surface of the river
                                   it's almost like dancing

it's still a passage of the real
time is less than time is more than
it isn't restitution but shorter than itself

                    as if we were adorned with numbers
                         as if sounds remembered this
                          the present seems to have passed

the pain in my shoulder remains
all the joins in the sentence
connect to the sun and the sky

                  air is variance, different fences, different acts
                        growth isn't simply a carnival
                    the next day things need to be done

tastes are never strange
they've passed me before
purpose freshens me up

                  sound is everywhere, in nests of dust
                      in the tentativeness of the sun
                      but where should I take the cold?

I bend down to listen, discarded hair
sings under canopies, kindness, shadows
a day quickens with darkness

Stranger Hat Cloud

The day has its hat
a trolley of clouds
strangers are shining
in a rain of votes
bring me shady dollars
and cards from the trees
we kiss
the unusual humidity
nothing is similar
but the same old wind
stinking up snacks
and yesterday's coffee

I can't get rid of all my ughs
but you   stranger   hat
day   cloud   trolley
but you dissimilar
were never forecast
and if you're not on the list
how can we manage
the trot through the car park

our brash foods aren't fair all those
rough lozenges all that
arch bling shouting
where's your nuts, your fruits
over the loom of your teeth

where's the intercession
in all the daylight crevices
on public benches
in the future where love
is difficult in a chapeau
the dead can't wear

Cirque du Suburbia

The thing you think of is jangling the breastbone.
You don't splurge or heave but it threatens like morning.

Someone's been hiding the ducks and tangling the burbsong
almost in jest, chirpy-chirpy cheep-cheep, as nuts with guns
short cut down classy streets with beautiful mullets and
    nipples.

The whole town is tempted onto the showboat, even I
am drooling about the new weather, the way Ray-Bans
fit an image that's deceased or a tiara if you need
an unhealthy respect for precious minerals, abandoned
    atmospheres
misreading the lux aeterna through a plain curtain.

Nothing repeats like television or spaghetti, we're told to
save it with our golden slumbers weighing more than you
    think.

Verisimilitude seems like a good idea until
the autumn snow of tax deals starts hackling the yard.

'Teen Charged with Attempted Murder'

The cops stare at the ground
mess splayed around the empty plaza

All this waiting here too for plants

Among the pink bottlebrush bees carry
bright yellow pollen   Is it heavy?

'It's what you're brought up with'

My shirt looks like some team's colours
if you mistake blue for black

Two old guys in the front yard
rake coals, prepare a raw dead animal
for the spit   cartons of wine

The teen was carrying 'some kind of weapon'
Perhaps it's what we now call a gun

I am trying to ignore football mania

We found one dead bee in the birdbath
and we were sad

'a history of mental illness'

'Are you a Richmond supporter?'

We don't want more bees dying

'recklessly'   so they tasered him

Under the Fountain

I walk on clinker and gypsum.
I pass by embankments, lilacs
and episodes. The air drones.
Everything is second-hand now
or untouchable, and was
once something else
even as apparition or feeble apology
a blue jacket sliding off
the back of a chair
a taxi door, and the way
things go
like clover, fire drills,
political scandal, faint music
the obvious speech
of the moment.

We cut down trees
to build bridges
fences are lies, so are fires
if you don't understand
if honesty is a convenience
like a plastic bag.
There are no memorials.
There should be
but what would they mean
if old age is the backward glance
just like your old town
or your skin.

And skin is everywhere, talking.
My lack of daring doesn't surprise me
but here I am
thinking how I could touch
more than is possible
even with all eyes upon me.
I am steely, sober, alive
among smoky columns
hungry torsos, hunched-up birds
under the fountain.

And all the speaking
rushing from me.

The Quality of Light

The light comes and goes
like a cloudy day in the 80s
or maybe the 90s, but anyway
a past time, when there were wires
and the incandescent
and a playful sun.
Maybe even an Impressionist
as late as Monet would
recognise it, even as his
eyesight failed during WWI.
Even though he's long dead. But the sun,
the atmosphere, the clouds
I can see, any day I look up, are
there, and changing there
with or without me. With or
without me writing as though
they are there for me.
But I'm not there, in the letters
though I may scribe them
while drinking coffee or watching
turtle-doves running along
the top of the fence
as another truck slowly prints out
tyre tracks in the dust along the
new rail's construction corridor.

Ink impregnates paper.
That does not seem remarkable
and it's not, if the words
merely 'come'. Exhaust and clanging
compose the day, as well
as light. And I think the air has become
more opaque since the 90s, though it's still
full of movement, of wings
and sound, water, leaves, disgorgement.
In the birdbath there's a yellow leaf
clearer than in the ponds, I presume,
of Giverny, only 80 k from Paris
but a place I've never been, or
the nerve system of creeks leading into
the Torrens, or the oily wash
of Sydney Harbour.
Luminosity perhaps is a dream,
like travel, building, or words. It all
comes and goes, it is
as if it's happening, at least
that's the impression, like light
as so much fails.

An End of Flight

The bird trembles before it dies.
Why are you holding it?
You're in a strange land. The trees are dark.
The bird's colours are like your land
where you're also a stranger behind
the terrible glass walls that seem free and bright.

Darkness and light aren't simply arguments
about doors, shelter, a twilight
of fanciful beings, daubs of thought.
You don't know what this small parrot
heard, what it saw. Home and flight
aren't simply discourse or headlines.

Glass is composed by heat and sand
soda ash and limestone.
It's only so far flexible. It's cold. There's a mark
where the bird struck. It dies
and your hands tremble with stupidity.

You will go back out into a stranger's yard
to bury it. Their yard?
A borrowing. All concepts are theft.
Even the earth is no longer primeval
but roots tremble as the wind moves branches.

Borders are always moving.
Where will you dig?
Soon someone will come in.

There's nothing tidy in any of this.
Any moment it will rain.

This Could Take a While

How do you get through days
that have already curved too far?
There are imps on the roof
no bigger than skinks or sparrows.
Their clatter rises like irritant polls
civil nastiness.

Envious angels attend the gates
sneering moodily.
Ghosts leave towels on the floor.
I didn't know they got so damp.
I am stiff with peeping
and tardiness.

I am building a machine
to see round corners
and decipher poems.
It requires great pulleys
bourbon-soaked vats
a hidden shaft.
It's taking a while.

I squeeze by the minutes.
I lick their juices.
My head is wet as a ghost.
My bones are like imps.
Sparrows make their home
in my corrugations.

I don't believe in angels.
All they do is pester me.
I get through days moodily
as though time is disappearing
down a hidden shaft.
As though it's a sport.
As though some automaton
syncopates in the doorway.

Ghosts are drinking in the corner
deciphering poems
drunk as vats and angels
churning, cheering
disappearing.

I Am Brushing Myself

shed skin like roses   share genders like perfume
shed skin like the dying tree   the day like its roses

smell lemon-scented gum   smell lemon   lick
genders like the yellow lemons in my hand   the rose

petals   white pink and yellow   on my shoulders
brown bark skin   the day shares its genders

all over my hands   stickiness   a prickle
the bug's orange life   the stamen's saffron life

the rich black loam   the shaky leaf   green
milk cut   the dead gum bleeding away   sap life

as agendas blow away at my feet   the changing air
as the kids play   somewhere over   the dog next door

whimpers and air floats the day   I am brushing
myself within it   this petal   this dust that enters me

as I am less or more than   the human as if roses or lemon
-scented   or rainbow-winged   or diesel-fleshed   or

air trails of smoke   or neighbourhood cheers   or
the lost beetle among   whatever   leaves are left

whatever   grit is needed   in roots

I'm Hiding like a Teenager

Is this the place to add
the photograph of childhood
What if it left me dizzy again
or sweating within the plush of trees
lapping fruit unto sickness
all the la-la of yesteryear
snapshots in gold frames
paroxysms and skirts
ringing in the years

If I hid in the curtains
from symptoms of formality
If I was silly plus
combing the settee
for the profusion or the promise

'before this
things weren't
so bad'

But I hid like a child
near the shoulder of a road
I played with small pieces
of lustrous tar
in the scrabble I saw
the face of this stranger
I knew

She offered me a map
I thought was a gift
she was only asking the way
the eyes of the road's
dark edges disappearing
as I approached

I have always been silly
in curtains in corridors
in the middle of a kiss
at least
I see down the weather
press the glass
fall from the frame
I've made

The grass out here goes on

As if You'd Break

It's always windy here, you feel molecules
—but what of

        Someone rustles orders
—as if they'd break a certain kind of husk
& everyone here, with doubles, counterfeits
—but you don't mourn the self

You can change everything
& still not be yourself—

        Some days you think
we all might explode
Celebrate the instead &
—even if you refuse, you can wait

It's hard to lift your hand
but see, you do
& every child does

        Do we speak, can we
not mourn the self
& mountains, old rivers move past us
& perhaps you do, this if—

Brought into Morning

When you go together
tempered in sway, air
dark's sound, sky
dirt, the length of it
your skin absorbed

when cats are no longer
cute, night birds and
traffic are clear when
reason does not equal
clarity, or death time

when hunting time's
cast of the moon, heat
absence, when fences
don't matter, remembrances
rain as *penseroso*

when being human is
not the point, the world
fills with water or
darker materials, doubles
impossibles forgot

The Findings

Coming from the city I am never ready
blossoms pour like stars or plastic sparkle
I am never ready for the brown stripy rain
animals of trucks animals of smoke
in death the rodent bulges until it's gone
somewhere the dog is still hidden
though it pounds the fence with its findings
and I am never ready for it the findings
though I drop the urb at the corner
and could shout if I could what is it
with all you beige and cloudy hills
just you wait for night and all those stars

colder than anything that sparkles
colder than night.

Revenants

You read about visitants.
It's often hard to tell, sometimes
they're normal or green.
It doesn't much matter.
You see these things.
They appear as comments
updates, news items.
Nevertheless they record
something that's passed
by you, has moved on
from corners, billows
wobbly horizons, appearances
that years ago
someone may have said
were other-worldly
but you know
that shades of day, time,
make-up and skin are more
or less the way things appear.
Nothing more spooky than light
or iffiness that makes you
drop things, stutter over mistakes
as if time could be
anything but time
some thing that passes.

A Pain Around My Shoulders, as Ritual

I like the lawn's yellow flowers
Lovely weeds, welcome!
I presume it's seasonal
                    growth
Happy grass
as shadows recede in morning

Make sure the gate catches
The way requires obstacles
                    and rusty handles

Everywhere time is
the passing passes
        into the future, the past
not history that's made
            of what's counted
rather than what's dreamt
by everyone present
    the magic elements
        love and despair
            awe and boredom
or simply that pain
    around the shoulders
my own ritual like a brace
before gates and doors

Or repetitions
a sip of something else
the river's metal
its spume and shade
its spawn and bloom

Impossible Spaces

You arrive with blank prescriptions
loaves, green papers, popcorn

You cling like all colonials
to the enigma of lawns and fences

You crash across salt and pepper shakers
cheesecake, fake wood panelling, bitter crumpled dark

You growl into corridors, into tiny impossible spaces
of sway, of hollows, of souvenirs, you're in two places at once

You run up against these things, breaking plain truth
harsh, nasty, as tired, hurt as the rest

You contort between flashes of flight
wide awake, shaking

You crunch, you become
you heave, you panic, you start to consider

You start to weep
in the middle of the road

The Wall, the Door, the Rain

Though it's giddy under stars
especially when they fall

there's nothing I can claim
of this world someone keeps giving away.

No-one will own up.
Was it me in the alley, the spotlight, on the steps?

I pinned nothing on the wall, or the door.
I never touched the rain or the falling stars.

If I have not delivered I wasn't sent.
If I came it's not because I was broken, alarmed or bent.

I suppose it's me, no joke.
I shot the sheriff, the archduke.

I'm crammed with exhaust and borrowed plumage.
My doors rattle with random glee.

I wonder what I deny.
The layout of industrial parks, terror on repeat?

I'm white with entitlements and modern footwear.
Blasphemy accumulates in my dreams.

I toss a coin.
That does for today's news.

I am made of asteroids and numbers, of shining cold water
or, no, I'm not bright like that

though I'm almost like rain
and everywhere I am in chains.

Same Love Goes Harder

Crime boy   and the ire of Conservatives
a flop in the big top

Pornography is the critics' tip

I cracked down   body-shaming trouble
on the front line

The Ashes   a slum
but 'Same Love'   'go harder'

'there's no excuse'   for
Air France emergency and   alien
pictures   a flop   a crackdown

Sinister reality   fake geniuses
and Vettel's engine trouble

'Tweets from angry old white men'
makes the ire go harder

For arms sales   and Uber
'couldn't possibly comment'

Go postal   go harder

A flop   accusation   costly error

'Same Love' thousands march   make more
to the top of the charts

Survival polls 'hang the Tories'

Gay anthem   the power

I cracked the door
and the love goes harder

Magic Hurt

It seems like the outside is fighting.
All night wheels go round.
I dream of ice as though it's cold fantasy.
You know you've forgotten something.
The chatter goes on. Uncertainty is
kind of fun. It's like test cricket. And rain.

There are no amends. You could rant
instead. There's an ecstasy in the nothing.
The windowpane proves it.
What's the extent of hurt?
Something more for the scorecard.

The real time is the wrong time.
You know we're making this up.
It's no dawn chorus.
The cupboards are whiter than that.
I have to hold down the fear.
It's what keeps me going.

Have a look at us having a look!
It's twice the fun.
The air is magic. We live in it.
I put on my shoes. That seems logical.
The labels are hard to dispose of.
A bit like advice.

According to the maps it's getting worse.
You've even run out of melancholy.
And goon. There's cloud for a while
all kinds. I tear open the package.
I start to eat. It sometimes works
without a battery. Singing is better outside.

The machines begin.
They startle me with their beauty.

Wrack

which way are you facing as the street falls
trees burst, windows crack
the rust has no consciousness but it attacks
a load of pipes crashes from the roof rack
of the white car scraping the wall
out the back, pink balloons bounce
on each other like feral boobs doing that dance
to attract an exchange of cash, love, consumption
it's a gasgaspgrasp, and an old woman is aghast
staring up at the hills where the horizon's
gone black and the wind makes that evil dash
through your soul's soul, what is it? Mars attacks?
it's all brooding wrack or media flack, the rain
that never rains will rain and no attempt at
political hack will stop the weathering of weather
the tide comes, it's not going back

Loss and Gain

What is it, some tell or course in the day,
in the freckled concrete, that impedes
so even tearing cracks of the blind
won't fully increase singing elements
gully winds, or pigeoned excess?
The ground won't wait, it mulches
as streets shoot by with
carry in commerce, the exchanges
going further than windows or joists.

Get hold of the present, then, rip whatever
hums near your soul into your head
spacing the sieve sound from notes
to sway taste of click claws and any
plastic glass doodad of the real.

Things in Place

Plasterboard, macadam
    nylon
all stinking in
       downpour
Under the tree
   a dead bird

Lunatic leaves   tremulous dancing
     sky with its
       loops and fashions

Sure, the wings of a dove
    plenty here

Avenues hang
   days still have stickers on them
   each car is a portrait

There's a fluffy dog
    in the big man's hands
Another dog
   drops the ball
     couldn't be arsed

Bodies play across gestures
   the wind
     lifts them up
there's grit in my mouth

Crows meet on branches
    summer shade   summer long
Under the eaves
        an unfinished nest

You and I looser
        now
and fronds   unfurl

Along the road
      dry branches natter

The tyres are very new
      waiting for the lag

All the gas in the ground
      bubbles up
through soapy ideas

I take a picture of clouds
    They're almost
        terrifying

On the lawn
      burnt leaves chafe
before slow finishing twilight
    later, a small tinker of fireworks

        If stars aren't cool
        they look cool

On the table is
    an empty glass

Do you remember the bridges
        Do you remember the northern moon
            The water's getting wider
                and we're becoming rootless

Yet

There are too many boots and bad ideas
    at the door

Within the book
    is forgivable dust

I wipe the bench   set the locks
        and traps
I cast out the light
    talk through the storm

Water
        makes all this noise
as though it saves us

Every day is simply a sample

A fly in the room
    summer
        at least   apparently
        in this corner

Remember the famous duo
Dry Heat

'Perhaps it's time to think about mood'

Round Midnight

You're home again and things click, getting ready
along with the fridge door popping. Flames, fruit, tea leaves
and the sound of news pages turning side by side.

No longer is the kitchen a mournful song overlooking
the long backyard. Water hustles preparation and wine
is a song that doesn't need sipping, whether it's red
or just a riff we remember together. I'm OK – you know
I'll always say this – but each minute makes its point
and an hour belongs to time again. Not that sitting down with
the expanse around midnight is a pointless activity.

I've done those stretches and come up bold enough.
But now this window is ready to include our shoulders,
my timing, your newest narrative. No-one else
needs to know in what other ways we can excel.

Autobiography

The kicks are in the underground
in the womb spliced together
seasons white against backdrop icy
under the table as I'm forwarded
dripping skinny and human.

Above it all I dance breathing
even if I lack the will
my independence screens as though
the separations were like
day and night not the dusks.

A shimmer in time catches
at the caught words tear down days
heartbeat sample jump to top of the page
where the ache begins   again.

The cloud dawns wind rattling
my husks strings and universes
seem not unlike but the gate sticks
and green flakes the heart of the camellia
doubles over petal layers
peeling shadows down to where
words feel cold falling rain.

Undoing

The street is full of the night
The night obliterates the street

Or they become one
Almost the same
Or they part

Like fingers or no
Like parts of a song

The night can't write or sing
The street doesn't play
With this matter

The street has concrete and money
Cars full of political clout

The night uses up electricity
Uses up feelings, sight and glass

Where are the people
In the cars, in the glass

The political clout moves
Behind closed doors
Night and day

Two lovers approach the night
Or the street

This has always happened
Her face half-lit
Her face half-shadowed

They smell of the usual fevers or demands
They smell like strangers
Of night wood, and forgotten wells

They part the night or fingers
They are always undoing
Returning to an older politics

The lustrous

Possibly Yourself

What is unheard
still sings in its
traces
smoky cloudy
song of a bird
you can't hear
don't know
in the profligate
and profane
items so many items
news from not-news
stories boxes
plasticity
brambles curves
what you could
have called
your daughters
all their little ponies
extreme lives of cats
murmurs of the boutique
the swimming pool
good news of
the wrong hemline
lipstick jazz
chosen unlike
the bloody chirping dawn
sounds unwise
snakes in the yard
want to be left alone

but those cats are
jumping
on the crackling iron
on seashore sound
the roof guardians
up there somewhere
falling as light
does amongst the
ground grid
waiting for someone
you don't know
possibly yourself
hence
house insects
on the wall
no use hiding

anymore

walk into the hills
the weather grips
your
clothing

At Least Four Instances

how do you fend off   the sea
it will be here   if not forever
                    but as your fever
or your shadow   when you stop
               breathing

    do doors open   as they did
does your hand feel   the same
               in the night

it's not   necessarily   a question
        of listening quickly
                    or slowly

    there's a fluorescent glow   taxis are helpless
ancient women discuss
          meanings   the lines across
          their cheeks
the junk is cast
          plants are broken

    shake hands with destruction
walk into the place   marked with
                    gold and dung

if you gamble with fortune   fences smirk
               the mulch is full of earwigs

a group of men   looking at the broken road
as if it was a puzzle
        that will take days

the night has its cloud face
buildings are illuminated
                by tricksters

the avenue fills   with splendid proposals
        lollies on sticks   avidity and cream

there are three   creaking noises
                in the morning
and at least four instances where   the room was busted
        by night's computer fire

you start with
        a humble shell
men talk to you   they come and go
        this corridor
        becomes a question

perhaps you miss your moment
        so, leave by the stairs
        the caretaker watches you   children swing outside
someone shines a torch
        on the code

envelopes slip   speech crackles
        everyone has a theory
bark showers down from clouds

bricks get bitter

It May Only Take a Minute

years go by then minutes
a bag stands in the corner
full and empty

a table collects itself
minutes collect years
full of claims

a day knocks around
counting the offices
of derelict hours

years are pranks
or blindings that are chock
with the usual excuses

it may only take a minute
to unpack to open
the lucky dip

a corner recollects itself
years go by and only a minute
makes excuses

sit down at the table
sort the claims
sometimes the usual is lucky

days and nights knock
at the offices of neglect
you say the years as minutes

a bag stands in the corner
years are pranks
where the lucky dip

Let Loose Looks

A woman looks among
A tree looks like a woman looks
On a refuse looks with a salvage looks
After another looks along a shelf
Looks into a self looks
Between a path

Looks over an accident looks despite
A blood clot looks following an advance
Looks under a shoe
Looks minus a drink looks round
A dream looks on a handle
Looks past

A roundabout looks for a rescue
Looks without a ring
Looks opposite a conspiracy
Looks to a lamp looks since a wound looks
Amid two looks as what looks like looks

Self and branch and air and secret and a bloody mess
And beauty and what's left
To the children to the smell of sweat
Alongside the train with the fresh feet following a shot
And a muscle

Looks but a branch looks like a brand looks as a fire feels
	and looks
And the way through with the sign with the nothings
	among
The extras with variables with adoration with rain

Between latitudes via never-ending with a basket
With furlongs to markets among songs
And diversions with the hammer
With the weeds along the flesh
And vectors despite the bandages

Through the prism with chains
And with rather than outworn
Or nonsense or vicious or drastic

A garden tastes like a woman looks as looks let loose looks
To tastes as selves
Paths refuse wounds
Rescues sweats sweet

The Un-marvelling

How strange last night, I beheld your face, electric
with thought along with my unrest, alight and hollow
when the night trees shivered and the block
we walked seemed more cluttered than the road
we used to walk, where every little plot
and fence was tended, maybe we were too narrow
maybe we lost our hunger then to care or look
to stare at stars, to forget the way we marvelled
how their brightness could also seem soft
and how the moonlight would seem to strain
through the canopy no matter how intense or thick
how this strange loveliness may never come again
how I wanted something – something I never quite got.

This Quintessence of Dust

So, I'm orbiting around   an average star
climbing into my insignificance   I can clap
or tap dance, drum   in the ancient
rift valley, the breast   the eternal child
high kicking its way   past the heliotropic

cheer the beauty of   retrograde motion on
a tall clear night   Sirius and Canopus
close and high Crux   between the calculations
I don't understand relationships   past human, more
beautiful, more than true   but I write
poems for aliens to   bypass in their
own quintessence, the algebra   of dust, that
is outrageous, exponential, inexplicable   receding
     horizons, paradoxes
alone and not alone   and love will
(what will love do?)   (love will …)

There's nothing fair in   this, although brightness
equilibriums, fallings, wobbles, mean   we're not in
this quite together, though   we are brighter
than fair, it's not   just other-worldly entertainment

particles burn
a moon rises
predictions predict
earth was blue

Bohemian Rhapsody

You drove all night
following shooting stars

Take it easy, desperado
we're all wanderers again

Listen
there is sound out here

Let's spend the times
and the changes

You're a wave
so oscillate wildly

No dictation tests
in the moon glow

Once the oxygen's gone
the fun begins

In the cosmic ah-um
you're laughing

Remains remain after first thought
fades in millennia fever

Here are our thousand dances
so, don't be afraid

Viva, viva the real
and the nights together

Tests

Testing an idea while the wind blows
may make you shiver, perhaps
at midnight or near a gate

Be careful of little children
they may run far away from ideas or gates

Be careful with your sails, your signs, your saints
your flesh, your fabulous knits, your sports flags
they'll catch on too many ideas, or midnights

The kids are out there laughing
they're not little pets nor common garden blooms
they have secrets they've stopped telling
there's no need, you forget, and shiver

Don't thank me, it's not as if
I know anything worth knowing
it's not as if I heard it through the grapevine
the grapevine is ornamental and a bit dead

Anyway, my hearing's shot, I mouth truths
as if they're jokes, and lies as if they're news
That seems about right

All those ideas, tested into forgetting
all the signs now at sea, all the saints unravelling
on too many flights through the garden

The kids are cheering, and why wouldn't they
I'd be moonstruck if I was less impatient
I'd run too, and where I'd run
I have no idea, which seems about right

You could come too
to be unsheltered
to swerve like a game
to look up
to cause all that pain

Stains

Something leaks into the earth
outside your window.
You hear it at night or early morning.
You see how it stains the walls
and the concrete.

It's more than a dream.
You wake and feel it tickling
and grinding your skin and hair.
The problem is not about habit, exactly.
The night could free you
if it wasn't so cool, or so hot.

You can't escape your structure
but maybe you can distract the scaffold
and feed your tastes, your failed
breath and veins, nerves
that light up agony.

Falling is nothing like it, there's no
new fashion that can copy hurt.
Sometimes it's early.
The train rattles like your bones.
The train goes somewhere else.

There's nothing you can take
up a mountain, a mountain is a myth
and so is a path.
You sit and stand, nothing
makes a difference.

The times have become stiff
like drinks or drought, little deserts.
Lie down in the gutter.
Feel how it all comes back at you.

As Matter Arranges

A lonely blue
sky a page
in the day's graveness

Also fresh luck
rather than a germ
of shadowy yolk

Apricots fall are eaten
our hands gather
what joins the garden

Open out your arms
to sweetened air
and the war's pain

It quickly moves
into us then away
with wing's thought

A page's shadowy
grave thoughts and
luck's pain

Things I Learned in Bay 13A

That sleep is imagination and I was immaculate
within a hangar of flowers, but there's no time for food.
A kind of leverage is essential when sheets attract blood
and that accompanying shot of salt.
That youth falls off its stem, though rays of fraud
still promise the thought of juggling desires.

It's all about how your water runs
and how it's accepted on the charts, the noisy gauge
the stethoscope, that loss may be indistinguishable
in the day and a purged dial tone is normal.

What is scary, if the darkness that is being cannot die
nor will it change, though all are changed?
Despite chameleons breathing into ether, I find that
on this graph the image of my heart is there.

That sleep is a contract of itself although beauty
isn't right anymore, the cannula blooms a tattoo
within the shadow of my inner arm, how easy it is
to repeat 'British Constitution' when there is none.
That I know I'm here because today is any day, 1st of Feb
and unfortunately I know the prime minister's name.

Voiceless flowers throw out their odour between
the grossly sterile and a body's dutiful stench
the pressure of feet and agitated clips of papers
the incandescence of the asterisk.

A shed flower lies where water doesn't work, outside
there's no southerly nor change, the soft rope cries
I was the lucky dream, 'out of here', and on the script
how more machines will make my image there.

That sleep is neither fantasy nor sensible.
It is a shed flower that balances then falls to the left-
hand side, the sharp pleasure is a phantom
with a ruinous smile, but time seems a relative
of nobody here. There's a sideshow of blips and bings
on the monitors and the azure curtains take their turn
in each act of rays through crosshairs
onto hefted and wrapped glass plates.

Like understudy revenants in unknotted gowns, we're
waiting for some allegro of welcome breeze, a miracle
like air's sky blue, or cake, to multiply our breathing
with my slow heart, boom boom, they attempt to find delays
in the desiring damp of my jiggy pulses
as if looking inward I'd find my picture there.

Bent

I am history now
in the scales, the age of sounds
I make sense then drop it

It gets dirty, it breaks
the ants carry it

I am bent at the switch
my tapes of the archive decay
loops stutter glitch arias

I am bent at the floor
facts roll under the chair
little dust songs
or songs outside
the parrots know

and I am still my species
struck, listening

Cracks in Stars

I remember crackers and stars
I wanted foghorns
I wanted to be alone
I remember Kodachrome
I had a bear
I wanted a better bear
I had snaps
I saw lattice
And there was a green tank
I remember the yellow sock
I remember the chalk stain and the warning
I had an idea, a mouse, a daffodil
These were all pictures and places
I saw a green tunnel
I walked into the room at midnight and could not get out
I remember an argument and stairs
I had a case
I assume I was there
I remember a driveway, a peach tree, privet and plum
These were all things, even the argument
I was outside
I was ill under the trees, as though
I'd always been there
    with these things, these sounds
A slide show on a wall
A stain, a tide, the cracks
    in some place larger than the world

To Hold onto a Map

To be out of place and to know that other place
is still there on a coast, to remember the colours
of a ridge, now velvet green in memory, to walk
in disparity with the colours of this place
and to know here too everything
is displaced and skewed with recall, to gamble
with timetables, to misunderstand lineages
within veils of tenderness behind doors,
to argue with the bondage of the breast, to flinch
while witnessing the bruise in morning, to wake
without meaning in an incredible blue heat,
to be disturbed by the advantages of blue
that test the eyes and in
turn veil them in unwanted haze
as though this was a memory bordering on
recall, to appear to die or faint in the straightness
of a road, to adduce this is a way
of describing this place, and to realise the world
moves a little east of itself when elsewhere, and to move
    with it, to be
    unbecoming
almost casually, to be less casual especially within
the darkness veiling the incredible lostness brought here
by travellers out of deserts, out of oceans, out of
indescribable histories, with bruises that make bodies
faint with remembrance, to apprehend an unbecoming
fear that swells lines of buildings, to discuss windows as if
they could see back into an original place, to encounter
sun like a glassy star on a balcony, to appreciate the aqua

dip of stairwells, to stare into the well, to test
absence, to walk a little slowly within a road
while green parrots skew the sound
of trucks and warehouses into the very
wildness that is now transported or dried out
along abandoned riverbeds and unwanted plains,
and to be followed by a slowness
that now echoes with finitude, to wonder
how that would operate as a sound once familiar,
    memory sharp,
     a blaze in the eyes,
burning leaves along ridges of the hills
stretching into the exactly blue sky dome, to wish
for clouds, and to know weather is not
will, to misunderstand distances, to understand how
the living and the dead wander
out of history no longer dreamt, to reject
the bonds of city lore without realising how
it holds things in places that touch each other
in the tenderness of finitude, to recant
    slightly
and thereby avoid tripping,
and to undertake wide streets in the blessedness
of time passing, to know how this place
is, and to lose the gamble with weather and time,
to uninstall memory, the taste of the breast,
to fold and unfold every map, to explore
the wrinkle and fray, the lost timetable
with its excuses for tickets, to finally turn
the corner, to find a place to live and work, that
    is the end
     to everything.

This is Not a Cosmic Poem

Everyone's gone home to write poetry
or soak their socks. The Milky Way gets fainter.
There's a party of shades on the path.
I might not write poetry about any of that.
I'll stay awake. It's hardly an effort.
There's something friendly inside the dark.
It's always been there although it's not
the same. Nothing is. It helps me see.
I can't write poetry about it but I will not
part with it. There's something fantastic
when light has gone, almost gone.
It makes everything sound clear. I understand
why you might want to wash things
at midnight as if starlight or moonlight
could make your clothes feel fresh,
sprinkled with expectation.
I imagine my body wearing a cosmic glow
that you could not put into a poem.
No-one would believe it.
Don't take my darkness from me.
When I get home it reminds me, even my skin
came from somewhere nowhere special.
Of course I'm like everyone writing poems
thinking my way from the light
and taking my socks off after
walking so far.

Grapple

Written on sheet sweat
thick thought waking
puffy sleep tricks.

Dreams lean as leopards
hunting & thieving
dance edges wild.

Your tongue fills out
the balloon, no, not this one.

(Those rooms in a building
stairs, dirty bathrooms
& something you'd forgotten.)

Get out of the plumbing & into the trees!

Sun plants delicate kisses
on the window
we grab it, shatter old air

grapple on the grass.

Get Up. Now

Within this hour you're fed up
with all your loading and the taste
of your sap curdled
around the stepping stones
you dropped yesterday in your
absences c'mon tell off time
tell off reason get up now
here's the curved hull of rubble
your own to climb start
rendering mingle it's warm
forget clarity tell reason that's
for lamps it's never been so porous
suck up the dirty old rain
it's not for you but there it is
step on it the present soil has
landed and caught you muffled
again learn from your rips and chagrins
stop waiting for progenitors or
consenting laser beams snap on
amaze the dead wood adults
are for the taking rake the yard's
stipple with your cold cold fingers
simplicity is confusing
decomposing on the ground.

With Our Shoulders

We are all making works I hear
us in the fences the metal
quavers and muddle tumbles
in time with our hands and
our breaths we make a blow
or a tough thumb into patches
of water grass cotton cement
parsley phrases gas conversation
we have tools of self-worth big crunch
and the absences of the wheel
o we are rolling our high
pitched handles and pulses
wheezing even as we hang
walls and move votives around detours
or heave loins and icicles
as if it's not a question of
happiness or learning flight
although coverts involve themselves
at heft and in the build
strokes through the breath
but if we are yet to be
skeletons we are still yet
to be making because
and there is nothing, nothing
without this bread, if fresh
burnt mould dry delicious
with our shoulders.

The End of May

The courtyard sounds sloppy with rain.
The sun is there always, but behind darkening clouds.
There's a mess of green and yellow on trees and paving.
It's nearly 11am and still not warmed.
Traffic stutters on North Terrace.
The oak leaves are familiar but wrongly exotic.

Hear all that sound, which isn't the little city
though it chugs and plugs away on slippy streets
but all that sound, as birds gather
lorikeets near sparrows, magpies near turtle-doves
all that sound of all those birds all the time
making curves and swathes and jokes of the squares
the city persists into though they don't really work.

I guess all the machines moving are also important
even what I'm doing is probably important, to someone.
It's decisions and numbers, while the ticking of a truck
backing into a space someone wants it to be in
makes it seem fresh and real and busy
inside and outside. Then the bloke in the truck
gets down and has words with another bloke.

I have words too, checking them on pages
as if getting past each line or sentence is something
achieved or, that's right, important.
The men give it up and begin unloading with
that metal sound of purpose and quota.
It's still cold and slippery out in this world.
Still and always full of bird calls.

That the leaves are also shining today.
That there's still a golden sense in greying stonework
of the early twentieth-century building
in one corner of the courtyard.
That there's still dust on the plate glass windows opposite
and they never seem to change in any light.
That birds in all this time will sing longer than
the courtyard and the desk, the buildings and the squares.
That this doesn't matter, that it does.

Small Things

Everything suggested has been removed
apart from a few pharmaceuticals.

The smallest things give form to light
beaten with wings, water-thrashed sky.

Each day thinks through frail modernities,
dangerous traffic, skin-filled impatience.

Hear the smoky breath of daily nostalgia
dreamt in Australian ways.

In the name of television, the news is bad news.
Each second gets a bit tricky.

Instead of a dove-grey rapture
wake up and arrange your resistance.

Alarms

Miracles are not like tempests.
Furlongs are not like hedgerows
though they come close.

Refrigerators are not like alarms
although propositions are tempting.

I am not above challenges
although grey kittens can be notorious
when hackers are around.

Tempests are not like refrigerators
though they come close.

When food moves, you move with it.
When it stops, you die alone.
Your fur moves onto another inventory.

It's tempting to alarm hedgerows
they're full of hackers eating hackers.
The kittens fall about.

Perhaps fur is a price
though it doesn't come close.

Break on Through

I remember part of my bootleg
something boiling over
but someone still had
an eye on the game
the serene, small television
I was original mono
someone was singing
like milk happening
psychedelic ball pock bang
the dogs were touching
things with changelings
charged with damages emptying
the fire extinguisher
into the ashtray I'm taking
notes then must sing them
expedition to a place
where I can think
the end being the apex
hypnotic sound from
someone's hands on
the vox turned low
I remember being
pulled down a road
I had to stop miming
my watch though
time keeps going
begins to end static
wires tubes and batteries
only present crackles

within the harmonium
and sublime's shaky hands
I was original bootleg
vox hypno and charge

The Soul of Things, DIY Sounds, and the Thin Eucalypt Rattle

To wish I could state something not in words
but in sounds, of the road humps as beats, insistence, even
sweet monotony, in the thin eucalypt leaves that rattle, a
    train's blast,
or the clear clean sound of late 50s Blue Note recordings
in my ears, or the clatter in my throat on a late winter
    morning,
muffled doof from a nearby car.

You could wish forever, all I have is bad timing, a ballpoint,
headphones, the trailing note off Tomasz Stańko then
a Brasil '66 segue, 'Mas Que Nada', voice, voices, samba,
    samba,
finger clicking, the cymbals are not leaves, this isn't Rio
or New York, not even Kansas or Sydney.

The magpie on the verge next to Greenhill Road knows
    that.
It's not singing, it's looking for what it's looking for. Food
is a solution to hunger and maybe creation. The hungry die.
There's no victory in metaphor. My body is full of itself
including breakfast. I'm still agnostic about almond milk,
it's hardly soul food. Milking almonds, gosh,
it's a long way from DIY or the sound of air through leaves
way back there near the Showgrounds.

Or what Herbie Hancock's *Head Hunters* album
has to do with any of this, synths, jazz machines, or the
    sound
of cranes above a construction site, winches, the cracks
in my useless knees, the smell of a city's early spring, pollen,
the sloopy offbeat of my foolish heart.

Bitumen Time

When you go home in dark,
when the street sings, bitumen thing,
or you, yourself, sing
this like birds, this like moths, don't
let anyone sing it for you
or anyone tell you, other than
this is whatever you make in the dark,
wherever you take this in the morning, because
there were things felt, times, places,
minutes that knocked, 'things that did not matter',
they do, of course, they do,
sounds that curve, drift down the long dark, a type
of sky song, hardness, cement walk, where
you trip, where the roses are stripped
of winter colour, indeed, who am I among
scent of this night flowering in dead arms of winter, so,
who can compare me, who softens me, is it
like childhood, as though history ramps into
the moon's famous indifference, the sky's
night version of real things that hold into
strange corners, so help me, help me,
it's transparent, but so alien, all these stories
I'm told before time rushes on
covering its angles.

Restless

I'm restless about affinity   There's a form
of am in every dream   Stress prevaricates
Aniseed lingers   You can be too fond of fences
making shiny choruses   Air is a treasury
The horizon fills with   shallow light
There's devil in the air   and everything's
forgettable or repeated   by cheerleaders

I failed at being   a host as crumbs kept falling
My wounds itch   on the right-hand side
and I made lines break   like bones
that made me reel

Form is simply vanity   I contemplate the heart
of each vegetable   How do you say what to say
Genius is like terror   You can never be that jolly
with scattered feet   The old bush had to be dug up
There's too much noise   Worry is a form of idealism

I fret each dirty line   The horizon fills
with self regard or   the last light on the gum
which is a pink glow you can   only see

I revise my chemistry   I argue with stairs

This Old Heart of Mine

Don't scrounge, my heart, leave the pickings
for the birds, there's always a magpie or
honeyeater who can use it better than you.
Just keep beating, flapping your valves
you old scar, make it seem effortless
like swallowing or taking or leaving
the minutiae or the passions, you don't need
to smile but you also don't need a gun or a plan
just your hands though they work badly.
Even the birds let things slip, cats drop
their prey, leave it for the ground, you've done
enough to the ground, simply walk
as though you are walking away.
What kind of reveries do you think you deserve?

The Sweet Space

Some days I'm here, some days I'm gone,
stumbling about that sweet space between
rooms, not a castaway, not a trickster
of those early morning dreams
who still accuses another from another
time of leaving the room too early, not
an inscription, grave or plaint
in the moon-myth light I could almost
believe, were I a believer in stars
heisted through a window, a lightfoot
mistaken in time, stronger than shadow
but, all the same, not the same
as I once came in the room, shouldering some
kind of burden, not quite the truth, the whole story, but
this real second, as divisions merge, as time
runs away with the spoon, the soup, the drug,
whatever's soothing, to arrange datelines
so you're out of it
's calculus of woozy syntaxes, gabfests
covering lies, time passing along the needs
for another story, but one plus one doesn't get you
one, get you out of here, whatever
they call it, here, meters tick, caskets
are laid, and someone, not me, chucks
a wheelie at the bend, as if the car's out of control,
which isn't a sign of anything else,
though the screech is now in the mind,
while I've got beyond
what I was saying, which had nothing

to do with where I was going, but look
ahead, there's expectation wearing its mask,
as if I'm a peddler of jingles and woes, schlepping
the ridgy-didge.

Notes

p. 4   'Swoop': The text consists of my 'half' of a renga-style poem written in collaboration with Andrew Burke in 2013. The full collaboration is titled 'Fiddlestick Nest' and appears as such in Andrew's book, *One Hour Seeds Another*, Walleah Press, 2014. This poem is, clearly, not in renga style, and a few of the original lines are reordered.

p. 16   'My Daylight Savings': The quote 'All Nature seems at work' is from Samuel Taylor Coleridge's 'Work Without Hope'.

p. 19   'Bad Sphere Dust-up': A longer and slightly different version of this poem was published in the magazine, *Dinner*, ed Sam Langer, Berlin, 2017.

p. 43   'I Am Brushing Myself': The 'lost beetle' is for Cameron Lowe.

p. 52   'Impossible Spaces': Every word and/or phrase in this poem occurs across various poems in my first book, *The Mask and the Jagged Star*, Hazard Press, 1992.

p. 61   'Things in Place': The final line quotes a remark from a talk given by Kate Lilley at the Experimentalities symposium, University of Adelaide, September 2015.

p. 78   'This Quintessence of Dust': The title is quoted from Shakespeare, *Hamlet*, Act 2, Scene 2.

p. 86   'Things I Learned in Bay 13A': Bay 13A is, or was, one of the smallest curtained spaces in Sydney's Royal

Prince Alfred Hospital Emergency Department. Patients who have experienced seizure-like symptoms are asked to name the prime minister and to repeat a number of phrases including 'British Constitution' (which is non-existent as a single document, of course). My birthdate is a 13th.

p. 102 'The Soul of Things, DIY Sounds, and the Thin Eucalypt Rattle': 'Soul of Things' is a 2001 album by the Tomasz Stańko Quartet.

Acknowledgements

I acknowledge the Kaurna people, the traditional owners of the country where most of these poems were written and where this manuscript was put together. I extend my respects to their Elders, past, present and future. I also acknowledge the Eora people on whose country a few other (earlier) poems were first written, and also extend my respects to their Elders, past, present and future.

A number of the poems in this book were first published in various print or online periodicals and anthologies, some in different forms and/or with different titles. I would like to thank the editors of the following:

4W, Arc (Canada), *Australian Book Review, Australian Poetry Journal, Bent Street, Contemporary Australian Feminist Poetry* (eds Jessica L. Wilkinson and Bonny Cassidy, Hunter Publishing, 2016), *Cordite Poetry Review, The Diamond and the Thief, The Eyewear Review* (UK), *Famous Reporter, foam:e, Glasgow Review of Books* (UK), *Island, Jacket, Journal of Poetics Research, Meanjin, Otoliths, Rabbit, Shampoo* (USA), *Shearsman* (UK), *Southerly, Stilts, The Stinging Fly* (Ireland), *Truck* (USA), *Westerly, Wildness* (UK), *The Wombat Vedas: Newcastle Poetry Prize Anthology 2011.*

'Swoop', 'The Quality of Light', 'Revenants', 'Wrack', 'Things I Learned in Bay 13A', 'Cracks in Stars', ' This is Not a Cosmic Poem', 'Bitumen Time' also appeared in the chapbook *The Quality of Light and other poems*, Garron Press, Adelaide, 2017.

'The Make-Do', 'The Wall, the Door, the Rain', 'The End of May' first appeared in the chapbook *The Leaves Are My Sisters*, Little Windows Press, Adelaide, 2016.

'Temper' and 'Bent' first appeared online as part of the *Australian Book Review*'s States of Poetry Series One in 2016. 'Bent' also appeared in the March 2016 print edition of *Australian Book Review*.

'Stranger Hat Cloud', 'The Findings', 'Get Up. Now', 'With Our Shoulders', as untitled poems, also appeared in the chapbook *Senses Working Out*, Vagabond Press, Sydney, 2012.

'Break on Through' also appeared in *The Best Australian Poems 2011*, ed John Tranter, Black Inc., 2011.

'The Quality of Light' also appeared in *The Best Australian Poems 2014*, ed Geoff Page, Black Inc., 2014.

Many thanks to Hoa Nguyen who provided advice and feedback on a few of the more recent poems in this book. Thanks to Ken Bolton, whose long-running series of Lee Marvin readings in Adelaide was a generous proving ground for early versions of a few of these poems. My grateful thanks to UQP for supporting Australian poetry and for taking this book on, with very special thanks to Felicity Plunkett for helping me see the shape of this more clearly and for her perceptive, responsive and careful editing, and to Madonna Duffy, Felicity Dunning and the rest of the UQP team for their supportive care for this book. As always, my abiding thanks to Annette Willis, for ideas, understanding and, most importantly, constant love.